Original title:
Blackberry Ballads

Copyright © 2025 Creative Arts Management OÜ
All rights reserved.

Author: Rafael Sterling
ISBN HARDBACK: 978-1-80567-246-3
ISBN PAPERBACK: 978-1-80567-545-7

Shadows in the Midnight Orchard

In the dark where shadows play,
Berries hide, well out of sway.
A raccoon dances, quite the sight,
Stealing fruits under the moonlight.

Giggles echo through the trees,
As squirrels plot with nimble ease.
Each berry plucked brings a cheer,
'Til one falls, and oh dear, oh dear!

The Elusive Fruit

Chasing dreams in berry land,
I reach out with a hopeful hand.
But every time I make my grab,
The sneaky fruit's a clever slab!

I trek through thorns and vines anew,
That juicy prize slips right on through.
Laughter spills as I trip and tumble,
For this fruit's got me in a jumble!

Beneath the Berry Sky

Beneath a sky of vibrant hue,
I spy a fruit with morning dew.
It rolls away with cheeky pride,
And leaves me flailing, eyes wide!

With friends I plot a berry heist,
We'll gather love, be sweet and spliced.
But every bite brings forth a laugh,
As juice drips down, we face the wrath!

Vine and Verse

A tangled vine tells tales of fun,
Of little adventures under the sun.
With every pluck, a giggle grows,
As fruit escapes beneath our toes.

Whispers float on winds so sweet,
Of berry wars and berry treat.
In this merry land, we play and jest,
Finding joy in a berry quest!

The Weight of Sweetness

Plump and round, oh what a sight,
Dragging my basket, with all my might.
Juicy treasures, I can't resist,
But why's my shirt now covered in mist?

Fingers stained, like they've been in fight,
Each berry taunts, 'You can't eat right!'
With every bite, my joy ascends,
A sticky mess with berry friends.

Thorns and Lullabies

In the wild where the berries grow,
I sing lullabies to the thorns below.
They prick and poke, but I hum with glee,
What sweet revenge, they can't stop me!

A thorny note, sharp and bold,
For every sweet fruit, a tale retold.
I tango with brambles in the sun,
Count my scratches—oh, what fun!

Chronicles of the Juicy Thicket

In the thicket where mischief plays,
Berries burst in clumsy ways.
Sticky pages of berry lore,
Each nibble opens a new door.

Now sugar-coated and slightly whacked,
I narrate tales of how I cracked.
With every splash of violet bliss,
Life's a comedy—I can't resist.

Nightfall in the Berry Grove

When night falls, the berries glow,
Like stars they shine, in moonlight's flow.
I dance among them, free and wild,
Laughing as I trip—oh, how I'm riled!

The night's a chorus, sweet and bright,
With berries playfully sparking light.
A funny feast beneath the sky,
With chuckles echoing, oh my, oh my!

Tales from the Berry Patch

In the patch with squishy shoes,
We danced along, singing the blues.
A squirrel stole our snack, oh dear,
We laughed and chased him without fear.

The bushes rustled, a bee flew past,
We whacked the air, a wild contrast.
A pie was thrown, oh what a sight,
We ended up in a berry fight!

Lament of the Bramble

The brambles are sharp, and so am I,
They tug at my clothes as I wander by.
A berry's ripe, it winks at me,
But oh the thorns—a tragedy!

With twigs in my hair and juice on my chin,
I thought this was fun, where do I begin?
I'll roast these berries on a hot summer night,
Maybe the bugs won't join in the bite!

Echoes in the Orchard

In the orchard's glow, we played on swings,
Singing of berries and funny things.
The apples rolled, oh what a mess,
While laughter twinkled in every guess.

We found a frog, with a berry-stained tongue,
He croaked our tune—it was wildly sung.
With every hop and every jest,
Summer evenings truly are the best!

Secrets of the Twilight Grove

In twilight's grip, the secrets spill,
A berry feast we can't fulfill.
The raccoon sneaks, oh what a show,
We giggle and whisper, 'Where did he go?'

The shadows dance, the glowworms gleam,
With berry-stained faces, we plot and scheme.
A prank on the owl, a berry surprise,
With a burst of laughter that lights up the skies!

Midnight Jam

In the moonlight, berries gleam,
A raccoon plots, or so it seems.
With tiny hands, he grabs a jar,
Turns midnight snack into a bazaar.

Marmalade dreams on toast so bright,
But who will clean this sticky sight?
With laughter ringing through the night,
We dance with jars, our hearts take flight.

The Deceptive Sweetness

Red and round, they lured my eye,
A tarty bite made me cry.
With unsuspecting glee I chewed,
That taste? A prank, I was booed!

Friends around me, in fits of glee,
As I wondered, 'What happened to me?'
While berries smiled, they had a plan,
To trick the hungry, a fruity scam.

Wild Harvest Serenade

Gather round, the sun's ablaze,
We scamper through this berry maze.
With baskets swinging, laughter loud,
In this sweet forest, we feel proud.

A sprinkle here and a splash of glee,
Who knew picking would feel so free?
With every berry, joy we find,
Singing sweet songs, hearts aligned.

Dusk Beneath the Canopy

Beneath the trees, as shadows creep,
We munch on berries, not a peep.
But watch your fingers, oh dear friend,
These juicy gems can cause a bend.

With smirks and giggles, we all share,
A squirt of juice, a berry flare.
As dusk descends, our fun won't quit,
A frolic here, a bite of wit.

Songs of the Harvest Moon

Under the moon, I danced with glee,
A pig in pajamas, oh woe is me.
The apples rolled, oh what a sight,
While squirrels plotted through the night.

Jars of jam and jars askew,
A sticky mess of sweet and blue.
We laughed as bees buzzed 'round our toes,
In the dance of fruits, the madness grows.

In the Heart of the Wild

In the woods, I met a hare,
Wearing silly shoes, without a care.
He winked and did a jiggly hop,
Chasing a fox, that wouldn't stop.

A raccoon played a tune on a tin,
While giggles echoed on the wind.
Mushrooms danced in their little shoes,
Under a sky that giggled and News!

Sugared Tongues and Starlit Skies

We licked the stars, oh what a taste,
Every single comet we embraced.
With tongues of sugar, laughter soared,
As moonbeams jigged on our dessert board.

We mused on life, with chuckles loud,
A pancake flip—a slapstick crowd.
The syrup dripped, a sticky fate,
In giggly delight, we celebrate.

The Delicate Thief's Journey

A thief so sly in a feathered cap,
Swiped a pie, what a crafty trap.
With wobbly knees, he dashed away,
Slipped on the berries, oh what a day!

He tripped on laughter, fell in a bush,
Squeezed out a guffaw with every hush.
His prize now a mash on his bum,
In the grand theft, how funny it's come!

Fables of the Untamed Orchard

In the orchard where shadows play,
The fruit laughs loud, come join the fray.
A wobbly squirrel with a berry hat,
Tells the tales of a jolly cat.

With whispers sweet and giggles bright,
The plump red stains bring pure delight.
A berry pie sings songs of cheer,
While the crickets dance, their rhythm clear.

Lyrical Forage

Oh, the treasure hidden near the thorns,
Where laughter sprinkles and mischief adorns.
A cheeky crow swoops low to tease,
Stealing berries with the greatest of ease.

The muddy shoes tell tales untold,
Of daring escapades in the bold.
With every squish beneath our feet,
We're artists crafting joy—what a treat!

Beneath the Veil of Leaves

Underneath the leafy dome,
A band of squirrels call it home.
With hats made of leaves, they sing and sway,
Writing their own berry ballet.

A rascal rabbit hops with flair,
Hiding treats everywhere.
Yet the chase leads to carrot pie,
As friends all laugh and watch him fly.

Rhapsody of the Dusky Berries

Dusky globes with mischief inside,
Join the dance, take a berry ride.
The jester owl hoots loud and clear,
Telling secrets that we all cheer.

Rolling down the hill with glee,
Staining clothes, just you and me.
While the evening sun paints it all,
We toast to fun at the fruit hall.

A Sweet Stain on the Soul

In the garden, berries burst,
A sticky hand, oh what a thirst.
My shirt now wears a purple hue,
Such joy in fruit, who knew it too?

Wiping fingers on my jeans,
A mischievous plot of berry scenes.
The dog just laughs at my disgrace,
As I try to scrub this berry race.

In every bite, a giggle waits,
Nature's trick, it tempts, it baits.
I chase the sweetness, what a ride,
With every stain, my heart's my guide.

The Longing of Wild Shadows

Beneath the dusk, the shadows play,
Wild whispers dance, come out to sway.
Oh, the moon finds us in laughter,
Chasing dreams we seek hereafter.

With every shift, the night's in bloom,
Berries scatter, we chase our doom.
Tickling whispers, giggles loud,
The night transforms our childhood crowd.

Branches rustle, secrets shared,
Each berry picked, a victory declared.
But watch the thorns, they seem to jest,
Prickly fun, put us to the test.

Harvesting Shadows

In fields of dusk, we paint the night,
With buckets ready, what a sight!
The berries beckon with a cheeky grin,
Let the harvest of laughter begin!

Stumbling through the bramble's clutch,
A giggle here, a berry touch.
The shadows tease with every fall,
What a joy to answer their call!

Our hands, a mess, like nature's art,
Each berry plucked warms the heart.
Who needs a basket when you have fun?
Play the fool, and let joy run!

Whispers of the Thorned Vine

The vines entangle, as we spy,
Berries glisten, beneath the sky.
With every pluck, a story told,
The tangy burst, worth more than gold.

But watch your step, the thorns delight,
In mischief's game, they bite tonight.
Laughter echoes, we dance in lines,
Funny how sweet's entwined with vines.

Collecting moments, as they cling,
In berry laughter, the shadows sing.
With every blush, the sweetness grows,
Nature's jest in playful throes.

Labyrinth of Wild Berries

In the brambles I took a leap,
Thought I'd find a berry to keep.
Slipped and slid through thorny trails,
Came out with stains and funny tales.

Berries danced with sugar's might,
Tickling my tongue, oh what a sight!
A squished one winked, said, "How do you do?"
Sassy fruits can be quite the crew!

I tripped on roots, screamed with glee,
Berries giggled, playing tricks on me.
Caught one, it plopped like a joke,
Making me feel like a cherry bloke!

At the end of this wacky ride,
I left with jams, and some berry pride.
Though I'm sticky from head to shoe,
I'd do it all again, berry crew!

The Melody of the Elderwood

In Elderwood where shadows play,
The berries rock in a grassy ballet.
Singing to the moon with a giggle,
Each berry bops, it's hard not to wiggle.

A squirrel joins in, with a fancy hat,
Twirls in circles, makes the forest chat.
"Catch me if you can," he squeaks and runs,
While acorns roll like buzzing guns!

A toad croaks loud, a boisterous beat,
Inviting all critters to dance on feet.
Under the stars, berries beam bright,
Making the night a comical sight!

As laughter echoes, the trees sway low,
Even the fireflies put on a show.
With every berry, a silly cheer,
Elderwood sings, bringing all near!

Interludes of the Bramble

Deep in the bramble where mischief lies,
Berries chuckle while the wild bird flies.
A raspberry said, "Try this, my friend!"
Turning my lunch into soft berry blend.

The brambles burst with giggling tunes,
Dancing with shadows beneath the moons.
Each berry peeks through the leafy glare,
Whispering secrets? Or is it just air?

A rogue blackberry rolled like a ball,
"Catch me!" it shouted, "I'm having a ball!"
I grabbed and slipped, fell into a vine,
Even the thorns seem to laugh, how divine!

Yet through the chaos, I cannot complain,
Each berry tale brings chuckles like rain.
Together we frolic, the thorns and the sweet,
In this wild bramble, life's quite the treat!

Tangled Tales of Autumn And Berries

In autumn's grip, where berries abound,
Tales get tangled, laughter is found.
An apple joked, "Why blush like that?"
While strawberries giggled and chatted like gnat.

A wise old crow cawed, "I've seen more days,
Than all these berries, in the sun's rays!"
Joking with crows, what an odd affair,
Berries burst out, like they don't have a care!

The pumpkins chimed in with a roly-poly joke,
"Who's rounder than me?" they happily spoke.
Berries were winks, their faces aglow,
In this riotous garden, laughter will grow!

As sunsets bathe the leaves red and gold,
The tales grow wild, never grow old.
In this bumpy brew of berry delight,
Fall whispers back, "Stay, it's all right!"

A Tapestry of Shadows

In the thicket, shadows play,
They dance and twirl, come what may.
A cat sneezes, a dog barks loud,
Nature's comedy, fresh and proud.

A crow with style, wearing a hat,
Claims he's the king, imagine that!
While squirrels dangle, like acrobats,
Stealing my snacks, those crafty rats.

The moon winks in a silly way,
As I trip over grass, oh, what a day!
Laughter echoes in the night,
As shadows giggle, filled with delight.

A tapestry of mischief spun,
Under the stars, oh what fun!
Nature's jesters, wild and free,
In this absurdity, just let it be.

The Lore of Hidden Delights

In the garden, secrets hide,
Giggles float with the morning tide.
A flower blushes, a bee insists,
"Sorry, dear friend, I can't be missed!"

The berries are plump, a feast in sight,
But watch out for the raccoon's bite!
His tiny paws cause such a mess,
He leaves me with berry-stained dress.

A worm in glasses makes a toast,
"To hidden delights, I raise a boast!"
Beware the ants in a conga line,
They slip on berries, oh, how they shine!

In every nook, joy does appear,
A tickled leaf, a buzzing cheer.
The lore of laughter, secrets unfold,
In nature's bounty, stories told.

Beneath the Veil of Leaves

Beneath the leaves, a party brews,
Frogs sing ballads in their shoes.
A shy snail peeks, then pulls back fast,
In this world, he's quite the outcast.

A hedgehog with glasses reads a book,
While twigs giggle, just come and look.
Dancing shadows, a critter show,
Watching it all, with glee, I glow.

The trees gossip in the evening light,
As fireflies spark like stars at night.
With every flicker, laughter grows,
In the whispers of dusk, joy flows.

Beneath the veil, the charm abounds,
Where laughter springs, and fun resounds.
In nature's arms, we find delight,
A vibrant serenade, pure and bright.

Bioluminescent Reflections

In the dusk, the glow starts to gleam,
A dance of lights, like a wild dream.
Fireflies twirl, a luminescent spree,
Whispering secrets, just you and me.

A fish in the pond dons a bright crown,
Winks at me, says, "Don't be a clown!"
While frogs croak in a jazzy beat,
Their rhythmic hops can't be beat.

The moon's a jester, laughing so loud,
Poking fun at us, a cheeky crowd.
The night blooms brightly, like candy floss,
Planting chuckles, no chance of loss.

Bioluminescent dreams unfold,
As nature's wonders continue to hold.
With giggling shadows and fanciful sights,
In this whimsical world, all feels right.

Whispers of Twilight Harvest

In the dusk, the berries gleam,
They tease us with a dream.
One poke and then a stumble,
Oh, how we laugh and tumble!

With each berry, a giggle loud,
Dancing under evening clouds.
Who knew that fruit could be so sly?
Just one bite and oh my, oh my!

We gather 'round the thorny brush,
In hopes of luck, we start to rush.
But watch your step, or you might find,
Sweetness lingers, but thorns unwind!

So here's to nights of fruity fun,
Harvest moon, let's all run!
For every laugh, and every sigh,
This berry feast lifts spirits high!

Sweet Danger of the Thorns

Oh sweet thorns, you sly little foes,
Temptation grows where no one knows.
A cluster ripe just out of reach,
With supple fruit, you start to breach.

We tiptoe close, our fingers twitch,
For that perfect berry, we'll risk the itch.
A tug, a pull, oh what a snap!
Turns a jolly jaunt to a berry trap!

Laughter echoes, as we retreat,
With scratched up hands and sticky feet.
For every berry that we adore,
There's a lesson learned to savor more!

So risk the thorns, embrace the jest,
In berry fields, we find our zest.
With sticky grins and tales galore,
Sweet danger calls us back for more!

Symphony of the Forest Bounty

In the woods, oh what a treat,
Nature's music soft and sweet.
Berries burst with every note,
Play this melody, let it float.

Our baskets sway to nature's song,
In this concert, we belong.
The laughter swirls with rustling leaves,
As we pick what nature gives.

Each juicy bite, a sudden cheer,
Filling our hearts with every year.
As night descends with such delight,
We jam and laugh 'til morning light!

So raise your voice, enjoy the cheer,
For every berry brings good cheer.
In this forest, we dance and play,
A berry tune that won't decay!

Garden of the Sweet Wild

In the garden where laughter grows,
Among the greens, the mischief flows.
With berries plump and leaves so bright,
We gather sparkles in the light.

Here's a berry, sweet and bold,
A daring taste, or so we're told.
But then a thorn gives quite a poke,
Oh what joy, and what a joke!

We race through rows, all wild and free,
Chasing giggles, you and me.
Who knew that nature's gift could tease?
With every bite, we feel the breeze.

So let's rejoice in nature's flair,
With berry stains and giggles rare.
In this garden, let spirits soar,
A wild adventure we all adore!

A Dance of Thorns and Light

In the garden where the thorns play,
The berries laugh, oh what a day!
A jig on the vine, they twist and sway,
Bringing smiles in a cheeky way.

With juice dribbling down the side,
These cheeky fruits take us for a ride.
They tease the bees, they run and hide,
In this merry dance, no need to bide.

Birds watch with envy from their perch,
As the fruits perform, a joyful lurch.
In this sweet trap, we all research,
The silly ways in which they search.

Under the sun, this wild affair,
Thorns tickle feet without a care.
In every twist, there's laughter to share,
Sweet berries banter in the summer air.

Serenade of the Berry Queen

Oh, Berry Queen with a crown of green,
You rule the patch, a sight unseen.
With every wave of your sweet sheen,
You conjure laughter, oh how serene!

The ants march in with a tiny beat,
Cheering for you, oh what a treat!
While squirrels gather, quick on their feet,
Making the most of your fruity feat.

With a wink and a splash of berry stew,
The butterflies dance, in a grand view.
In this whimsical realm, what to do?
Join the revelry, yes, me and you!

Under the moon, the night unfolds,
The Berry Queen's secret story told.
With giggles and grins, the world enfolds,
In a berry dream, we find pure gold.

Enchanted Orchard Reverie

In an orchard where giggles grow,
Fruits are pondering, oh what a show!
With every breeze, a secret flow,
Filling the air with joy, you know!

The plump ones whisper, sharing their tales,
Of fruity escapades and river trails.
While mischief-making, the surprise prevails,
As laughter echoes through leafy veils.

A squirrel pipes in with a cheeky jest,
Claiming his stash, he thinks he's the best.
But berries chuckle, they're not impressed,
In this enchanted place, we're all blessed.

As the sun dips low, the fun won't cease,
Orchards alive with joyful release.
In every corner, laughter's caprice,
An enchanted night, our sweet peace.

The Mystery of Sweet Eclipse

A shadow drapes on a sunny morn,
As berries giggle, their mischief born.
In light and dark, their riddle's worn,
What's troubling these fruits, so forlorn?

With a wink and a twist, juice takes flight,
As they tumble down, oh what a sight!
Bright smiles abound, banishing fright,
In this jester's dance, all wrongs make right.

The moon peeks out, casting a grin,
As harvest crew stumbles, laughter within.
Berry bandits plotting their win,
In the mystery of sweetness, we all spin.

Cackles and squeaks fill the bright skies,
As the fruits together, share their surprise.
In this delightful riddle, who can despise?
A tasty eclipse that never belies.

Serenity of the Berries

In the garden, berries stray,
Their sweet whispers come out to play.
Laughter floats on leaves so green,
Nature's little jester's scene.

With every bite, a burst of cheer,
Sticky fingers, never fear!
A comical dance, we spin and swirl,
As juice drips down and laughter unfurls.

The sun shines bright on frolic ground,
While squirrels watch without a sound.
A feast of laughter, in a bowl,
Rolling giggles make us whole.

So gather round, let the fun commence,
With berry antics, there's no pretense.
In this patch, joy reigns supreme,
A berry kingdom, a sweet dream.

Song of the Hidden Fruit

Beneath the leaves where shadows creep,
A fruit sings softly, secrets to keep.
In this patch, a treasure lies,
With giggles hidden, oh what a prize!

Nature's jesters, dark and round,
Plucking them brings joy profound.
A mischief-maker, stained with glee,
Berries dance in wild jubilee!

Watch the squirrels with their acorn stash,
Chasing berry dreams in a giddy dash.
The sun's warm kiss on a juicy bite,
Berry bliss makes the day feel bright!

Singing soft amid the green,
Nature's humor, sweet and keen.
Join the tune, let laughter ring,
In the woodland, merrily swing!

Nectar on the Breeze

The air is thick with sweet delight,
Berries laughing in the sunlight.
A breeze carries tales of charm,
Pulling friends in with its warm arm.

Buzzing bees are in a race,
Chasing nectar, quick in pace.
With each drop, a chuckle's found,
In the honeyed chaos, joy abounds!

A berry pickle, oh what a sight,
Stuck in bushes, in pure fright.
Pull them out with giggles bright,
Nature's pranksters, what a night!

Sipping laughter, tasting cheer,
With sticky fingers, hold them near.
In every bite a story's spun,
Underneath the glowing sun.

Grappling with the Wild

In the bramble, we take a stand,
With berry battles, laughter's planned.
Caught in thorns, we wiggle free,
As nature chuckles, wild and carefree!

Each berry scoffed, each berry snatched,
Our playful war is fully hatched.
With berry juice as our bright shield,
In tangled vines, we'll never yield!

Nature's jester in wild display,
As we grapple in the berry ballet.
With every fall, a silly grin,
It's fun and games on this sweet whim!

From forest floor to sunlit glade,
Each berry plucking an escapade.
So here's to laughter, wild and free,
In the berry patch, come and see!

The Berry Collector's Heart

In a field where berries grow,
He trips on roots, oh no, oh no!
With basket wide and hopes held high,
He dreams of pies beneath the sky.

But every berry in his clutch,
Is squished or stained, oh what a touch!
He cackles loud, his laughter bright,
This berry chase, a silly flight.

Each time he bends to pick a prize,
A bee says hi, much to his surprise!
He runs away, his treasures lost,
Oh, collecting berries comes at a cost.

Yet with each fall, he stands again,
His heart still wild, never a drain.
For in the muck, and in the mess,
He finds the joy, he finds the best.

Melodies of the Overgrown Path

Down the lane where bushes sway,
A bird sings loud, come what may.
The branches thick with berries sweet,
He skips along, oh what a feat!

His hat askew, he feels so fine,
A dance with nature, foot and vine.
A sliding slip, a tumble grand,
He's sipping juice while making sand.

But fret not friends, his tunes arise,
With fruity notes that fill the skies.
The path he treads, with giggles bright,
Is sprinkled with laughter's pure delight.

And when the day draws to its end,
He waves goodbye to every friend.
Melodies of bramble's song,
Are carried home, where they belong.

Gifts of the Bramble Thicket

In bramble thickets, secrets hide,
With fruits so ripe, oh what a ride!
A rummaging hand, a sneaky pluck,
He's on a quest, he's out of luck!

For every berry has its quirks,
A thorny dance that might just lurk.
He giggles loud, then struggles free,
Who knew a bush could laugh with glee?

He fills his arms with sticky loot,
But stumbles 'gainst his own big boot.
His friends all laugh, and pull him up,
As he spills juice, a berry cup!

Yet in that mess, his heart shines bright,
For every bruise is pure delight.
Gifts of thorns and fruit divine,
He'll tell the tale, of berry wine!

Ripe with Secrets

In the hush of morning's gleam,
He stumbles through the berry dream.
With vines entwined and jokes to tell,
He hushes now, to hear them well.

Oh secrets whispered by the breeze,
Tell tales of birds and buzzing bees.
He's on a hunt for sweet delight,
That leads him deeper into the night.

A rush of laughter fills the air,
As tangled limbs cause a wild scare.
He loses shoes and steals a bite,
His belly full, his heart alight!

With goofy grins and berry stains,
He's one with nature, wild and unchained.
Ripe with secrets, joy's own art,
He dances on, with a silly heart.

The Brush of Thorns

A thicket here, a poke there,
Those brambles laugh with glee.
In the quest for juicy treasures,
I trip and dance, oh me!

With purple stains on my hands,
I grin at the careless jest,
The vines conspire with the bees,
In this fruit-filled, thorny quest.

Each snag a playful tease,
As I reach for one more bite,
But alas, I've grabbed a thorn,
Oh what a silly sight!

Yet every berry gathered here,
Brings laughter to the day,
With friends who stumble and tumble,
In this wild, sticky play.

The Symphony of Aged Vines

A song of vines, so intertwined,
They whisper tales of yore.
With plump delights that hold the night,
They keep us wanting more.

The grapes all giggle, swaying low,
In the breeze, they take their stand.
While I try to catch the rhythm flip,
With berry juice in hand.

A little too much sway and spin,
I join their lively cheer,
A dance of clumsy berry choose,
While laughter fills the sphere.

Each sip a jolly reminder,
Of the mischief we have sown,
In the symphony of aged vines,
We're never all alone.

Fruits of the Wandering Soul

I wandered far to seek the sweet,
With dreams of every hue.
Yet in the woods, I lose my way,
And find confusion too.

A berry here, a vine misplaced,
It's like a maze, you see.
I try to gather every fruit,
But trip on roots with glee.

My basket spills, the fruit goes wild,
A gala in the grass,
While critters join in on the fun,
As I attempt to pass.

Though every berry found is grand,
I wear a crown of green,
A jester to the wandering soul,
In this fruity, merry scene.

Bards of the Berry Witch

Underneath the glowing moon,
The berries start to sing.
With every squish and every smash,
They welcome in the spring.

The berry witch, with cackles bright,
Concocts her berry brew,
And all the bards, with tails entwined,
Join in the merry crew.

They rhyme about the sticky nights,
Of feasts and fruity fights,
With laughter echoing through the woods,
In berry-tinted lights.

So raise your cups of purple soup,
And dance the night away,
For in the tale of berry bards,
We find our bright display.

The Twilight Orchard's Heart

In twilight's glow, the berries dance,
A raccoon prances with a sly glance.
The branches sway, all filled with glee,
As critters scheme for more than a spree.

A squirrel claims a throne of green,
While crows conspire, they're quite the scene.
They caw and cackle, plotting their feast,
While I just watch, my laughter increased.

Nature's jesters, they work so well,
Each berry snatched, a tale to tell.
In this orchard's heart, the laughter flows,
As night descends, the mischief grows.

With every ripple, joy takes flight,
In moonlit pranks that last through night.
The orchard thrives with jovial cheer,
Whispers of fun, the harvest near.

Chorus of the Berry-laden Breeze

The breeze hums sweet, a funny tune,
With berry vibes from sun to moon.
A dance of flavors, a laugh in the air,
    As critters gather without a care.

The dandelions giggle, the grass takes a bow,
While hungry bees buzz, oh, where are they now?
A chorus of chaos, the fruits all delight,
In nature's spectacle, everything's right.

The elder below plays a jester's part,
As the mischievous goats feast, oh, what an art!
Each nibble and munch, a cacophony grand,
An amusement of taste in this berry land.

Dance on, dear berries, with whimsy abound,
In breezy laughter, joy knows no bound.
A melody sweet beneath skies of blue,
As we all join in, for they're feasting too.

Interludes in the Bramble

In thickets of joy, the wild things roam,
With ripe little treasures far from home.
A fox with flair, in shades of tan,
Steals a sweet berry, like a berry fan!

The hedgehogs chuckle, the rabbits all grin,
As jellied delights make their world spin.
A tussle ensues, all in playful jest,
Nature's own pranks, this harvest is best!

A ladybug whispers, keeping it sly,
While a far-off crow tries to sing and fly.
Each verse of life in the bramble's embrace,
We pick and we laugh in this merry place.

They tumble and tumble, rolling in glee,
In the bramble's arms, they feel so free.
With flavors of joy, they feast and they play,
In intervals of laughter, they brighten the day.

Echoes of Ripe Abundance

The garden sings with echoes bold,
As sweetness drips from vines of gold.
Every laugh that lingers, a berry's song,
In this ripe abundance, we all belong.

The bees start a buzz, a mischievous crew,
Spreading the tales of the berry brew.
Chortles of critters fill the warm air,
In joyous abundance with laughter to share.

A festival blooms where the sunbeams play,
And jolly old squirrels scamper away.
They leap from the branches, a merry brigade,
In echoes of fun, every moment's made.

When the sun sets low, the laughter remains,
In whispers of berries, sweet joy sustains.
So gather close, let the echoes impart,
The fun never fades in the orchard's heart.

The Sweetness in the Shadows

In the shade where bushes grow,
I found a berry, oh what a show!
Plump and purple, bursting bright,
Made my fingers sticky, what a sight!

Laughter echoed through the grove,
As I slipped and fell, like a clumsy dove.
Neighbors chuckled, pointing, too,
"Berry picking should be left to you!"

The juice ran down my chin with glee,
I grinned and danced, so wild and free.
A berry tart was my grand plan,
But now I just resemble a fruit-filled man!

With each bite, a giggle unleashed,
Nature's candy at my feast.
The sweetness hid in shadows thick,
Who knew a berry could be so slick!

Tales from the Bramble Grove

Deep in the bramble, tales unfold,
Of berry bandits, brave and bold.
They sneak and peek, with cheeky grins,
In the battle of fruit, oh, let the fun begin!

One sly fox with paws of gold,
Swiped my stash, if truth be told.
He scampered off, the nerve of that fellow,
Leaving me with only a dark blue jello!

The rabbits hopped, they also stole,
Cunning critters, they take their toll.
With every nibble, giggles arise,
As I chase them under sunny skies!

In the heart of the grove, mischief thrives,
Berry brawls make for funny lives.
Join the party, don't be a bore,
In the bramble, laughter is never a chore!

Dreams Stained with Dark Juice

In my dreams, the berries reign,
Juicy visions drive me insane.
A crown of thorns, I wore with pride,
My throne a berry bush, where I'd reside.

The stains on my shirt tell tales of bliss,
Each juicy encounter, I can't dismiss.
But watch your step, or you might find,
A berry trap laid, not for the blind!

A dance of flavor, the critters knew,
They threw a party, in purple hue.
With every snack, I'd burst with cheer,
Who knew fruit could bring such a sphere?

In the dawn, friendships bloom anew,
With laughter sweet, and a hint of dew.
Dreams tarnished, but never a flaw,
Where darkness dwells, just laugh and guffaw!

Beneath the Canopy of Secrets

Beneath the leaves where shadows cling,
Lies a world of laughter, birds that sing.
The secrets of the grove unfold,
In juicy whispers, mysteries told.

A squirrel danced on a branch so high,
With a berry prize, catching my eye.
He wiggled his tail with a cheeky flair,
Dropping fruit, oh what a snare!

The gnome nearby snorted in bliss,
Caught off guard, I had to hiss!
With laughter bubbling, I raised my cheer,
What mischief brews in this berry sphere?

In the canopy where secrets play,
Funny tales brighten the darkest day.
So join the jest, and take a chance,
In this berry world, let's laugh and dance!

The Berry Connoisseur's Lament

Oh, taste the berry, sweet and wild,
But mind the thorns that make me riled.
A jam-jars' war, it seems to be,
Trapped in a bush, oh woe is me!

I dreamed of pies, so rich and grand,
Instead, I'm stuck in thorny land.
With fingers stained and face all smeared,
The neighbors laugh, my fate is cleared!

What joy it brings, this juicy fight,
I pluck and stumble, what a sight!
The fruit's allure, a siren's call,
Who knew the fun would hurt at all?

So here I stand, a berry fool,
In a patch that's no one's school.
I'll dance with thorns and share my plight,
For laughter's sweetness is pure delight!

Nightshade Melodies

In midnight's shade, the berries sing,
A tune that makes the crickets cling.
But heed the notes that lead you wrong,
For nightshade's laugh is quite a throng!

A berry feast within the dark,
With every bite, I miss the mark.
Oh, nectar sweet, you sly little tease,
A bit of bliss, a dash of wheeze!

The moonlit jam, it calls my name,
I dive right in, oh what a game!
Yet morning finds a funny twist,
I smile and sigh, it's berries missed!

So heed my song in cherry haze,
For every night, a tangled maze.
With giggles bright and belly sore,
I'll waltz with berries, evermore!

The Hidden Bounty

Out in the field, a treasure lies,
Hidden beneath the tangled spies.
I hunt with glee, a berry scout,
But here comes trouble, roundabout!

What joy to see a basket full,
Of plums and grapes—it pulls my wool.
Yet in the midst, oh bulky foe,
A chubby raccoon steals the show!

He's got my berries, cheeky bandit,
With beady eyes and nimble hand, it.
While I stand watching, jaw agape,
He dances off, a funny shape!

So here's to finds both sweet and sly,
With laughter's echo, I won't cry.
For every loss, a tale to spin,
In berry hunts, the fun's within!

A Dance Amongst the Thorns

Among the thorns, we spin and sway,
In berry dance, we find our way.
With petals soft as whispers fleet,
We giggle loud with thorny feet!

A twirl and dip, can't stop the plight,
My berry crown, a comical sight.
With every step, I slip and slide,
Yet with a laugh, I take it in stride!

The brambles laugh, they know the game,
Each berry snag is all the same.
We dance like fools beneath the sun,
Together tangled, oh what fun!

So here's to joy in every prickle,
With paint-stained fingers, what a trickle!
In laughter's arms, we find a home,
In dances sweet amongst the loam!

The Last Harvest Song

In a patch where berries swayed,
A squirrel danced, unafraid.
He thought he'd found a feast,
But tripped and flipped—what a beast!

Jars were lined upon the shelves,
Full of jam for folks and elves.
But one jar tipped, what a sight!
Blue splatters turned the world bright.

Neighbors came with spoons in hand,
To taste the fruits of the land.
Laughter rang out, joy was grand,
With sticky fingers close at hand.

So raise a cheer for that last jar,
Even if it became a star.
For in this berry-filled song,
We'll giggle and dance all night long!

Dawn Over the Wild Berries

At dawn, the dew was fresh and bright,
Berries glistened in morning light.
With baskets swinging, off we ran,
To pick our fill; oh, what a plan!

But as we searched for the best fruit,
A bear appeared, who was quite astute.
He showed us how to pick with flair,
While we just stood, caught unaware!

With berries strewn upon the ground,
We laughed at how the bear wrapped round.
He took our snacks, a cheeky thief,
While we just stood, sharing disbelief.

So here's to mornings, wild and free,
With berries, bears, and endless glee!
For every jammed mishap there's fun,
In the dance of dawn, we've all won!

Vintage of the Forest

In the forest, a secret found,
A vintage shop turned upside down.
With berry bottles, old and weird,
We set to taste—oh, how we cheered!

But one popped open like a champ,
Scent of berries, sweet and damp.
Our taste buds twirled in fright,
Was it jam or a frightful bite?

The old man chuckled from the door,
"Just a splash, not a bit more!"
With juicy laughs, we spilled and sang,
As berry bubbles burst with clang!

So raise a glass to forest finds,
With quirky tastes that make us blind.
For in this vintage tale we see,
The fun in flavors will always be!

A Mysterious Melody in the Vines

In the vine-clad maze, we lost our way,
Yet laughter echoed, come what may.
A tune floated down from the stars,
   Could it be from magical jars?

With berries bouncing along the path,
We danced and twirled, avoided the wrath.
By a gnarled tree, we found our beat,
And shoes flew off, that's how we meet!

Turns out the melody came from bees,
  Buzzing sweetly among the leaves.
We joined their song, a wild spree,
  With sticky fingers, oh, such glee!

So let the music guide your way,
Through berry trails where we will play.
For in the vines, where laughter sways,
  We find our joy in funny ways!

Dance of the Summer Harvest

In fields where the laughter springs,
Berries jiggle on leafy things.
A robin chirps a silly tune,
As sunbeams wink beneath the moon.

With baskets big and smiles wide,
We prance with joy, we won't just hide.
Staining fingers from sweet delight,
We twirl and dance in pure sunlight.

The squirrels glance with jealous eyes,
While we feast on nature's sweet surprise.
Oh what fun, this fruity spree,
A harvest dance for you and me.

So grab your hat and join the cheer,
Let's sing and laugh, the end is near.
With every bounce and every laugh,
Dance on, my friend, and take a whiff!

The Bramble's Embrace

Oh, tangled thorns and sweet delight,
In bramble's grasp, we find our flight.
With hands a-smeared and hearts so bold,
A funny tale of berries told.

Like ninjas swift through prickly lanes,
We dodge and weave, ignore the pains.
Each berry plucked is worth the fight,
A treasure found in playful light.

The tales of woe are quickly spun,
Of berry splats and races run.
With giggles echoing through the vale,
We share our spoils, we tell the tale.

So let the brambles tease and tickle,
As laughter rises, raucous and fickle.
In this embrace, we find our grace,
In every bruise, a smiling face!

Between the Vines

In shadows cast by leafy green,
We sneak a taste, oh what a scene!
The sun shines down, a cheeky grin,
As juice drips down from chin to skin.

We hide from folks who pass us by,
With berry roars and laughter high.
"Did you see that?" we weave our tales,
While munching on our fruity bales.

Reluctant bears, they hold a claim,
But we won't sell our joy for fame.
We're berry bandits without a care,
Between the vines, we dance and dare.

So come along and catch the thrill,
For in each bite, we find the chill.
With giggles shared, we'll make our stand,
Between the vines, a berry band!

Fragments of the Forgotten Orchard

Once overgrown, now a jewel bright,
Forgotten gem in morning light.
With laughter echoes through the trees,
The fruits are sweet, they aim to please.

We stumble o'er the roots and rocks,
With berry stains and mismatched socks.
Each laugh a melody anew,
In this sweet orchard, just me and you.

The fragments sing of days gone by,
Of secret feasts and silly sighs.
With every bite, our spirits soar,
In these wild fruits, we find the core.

So let's remember, dance and sing,
Through tangled paths, our joy we bring.
In laughter's glow, we find our way,
In nature's arms, we laugh and play!

Tides of Dusk and Berry

The sun dips low, a jeweled glow,
Berries burst in bloom's soft sigh.
A squirrel prances, with cheeky chances,
Steals my snack, oh my, oh my!

Laughter spills where shadows play,
Each berry squished, a fruity fight.
We dance around in dusk's bouquet,
Chasing giggles, hearts alight.

With every splash, the juice does stain,
Fingers purple, faces too.
The tide rolls in, a sweet refrain,
Nature's trick, so funny and true.

So raise a cup to cheer the night,
In jester's cap we toast to fun.
A berry bounty, pure delight,
Under the sky, our work is done.

The Unseen Harvest

In fields of green, where giggles lie,
The berries hide from prying eyes.
With each bold step, I poke and pry,
  Yet they giggle, oh how they rise!

A basket's full, or so I think,
Then comes a bird, with knowing glance.
It snickers loud, makes me blink,
While berries dance away in prance.

The wily critters plot and scheme,
  To steal away my juicy prize.
I chase them down, a comic dream,
While nature laughs and rolls her eyes.

But in this game, I'm still the king,
  With laughter ripe, my heart is free.
Though hidden gems make mischief sing,
  The joy's the harvest, wait and see.

A Lament in the Thicket

Oh, woe is me, I've lost my way,
Amongst the brambles, sharp and sly.
With every slip, I wail and sway,
"Why did I think this was a pie?"

My shirt is snagged, my shoe is stuck,
The berries mock with juicy glee.
Every twist, a twist of luck,
A berry thief, that's what I be!

Fingers stained in berry's hue,
I stumble forth, a ragged man.
The thicket holds its laughter true,
As nature plots its berry plan.

Yet in this plight, I find my mirth,
Beneath the thorns, a funny tale.
For every poke, there's berry worth,
In laughter's light, I shall prevail.

Secrets Buried Under Leaves

Beneath the leafy, leafy quilt,
Lie secrets sweet, of joys unspoken.
With stealthy hands, I gather guilt,
As berry dreams keep me awoken.

Each rustling leaf, a tale unfolds,
Of double dips and spilled delights.
The berries chuckle, brave and bold,
In secret quests of funny nights.

Stumbling through with berry squish,
I find my prize, then spill it quick.
The critters laugh, a berry wish,
And I, the clown, in nature's trick.

Yet buried deep in roots ya see,
The sweetest secrets made to tease.
So join the dance, come laugh with me,
In joy's embrace, we find our ease.

Threads of the Wild Harvest

In the thicket, berries gleam,
A jester's grin, like a dream.
Plucking fruits that dance on air,
Stains on shirts, without a care.

Chasing shadows, what a sight,
Berries spilled in pure delight.
Laughing pigs now join the race,
A fruit feast in this wild place.

The basket's full, yet so is my heart,
Nature's bounty, a laughing art.
The sun dips low, a golden cheer,
With every giggle, more berries here.

So we gather, sharing the fun,
Laughter ringing, never done.
With juice-stained hands, we celebrate,
A wild harvest, truly first-rate.

Nectar-Laden Dreams

Every night beneath the stars,
Dreams float in jars, like sweet bazars.
Juicy visions of fruit-filled skies,
Where laughter's nectar never dries.

In the morning, we rise with glee,
Syrup drips from each dreaming tree.
Smiles plastered on faces bright,
As berries tumble in morning light.

Frogs serenade with croaky tunes,
While bees bustle, collecting boons.
It's a symphony of buzzing fun,
As nectar flows, we laugh and run.

So here's to dreams, both sticky and sweet,
Life's quirks wrapped up in a berry treat.
With each bite, let the giggles rise,
In this nectar world, love never dies.

An Ode to the Thorny Path

Amidst the brambles, oh what fun,
A prickly path we wildly run.
Squeezed between thorns, oh dear me,
But laughter grows like a bushy tree.

With every poke, we dance and squeal,
Stumbling forth, a comical reel.
Wincing, laughing, our tales collide,
In the thorny maze, we take pride.

The juicy fruit hangs, just within reach,
A prize awaits, sweet lessons to teach.
We leap and bound, a merry spree,
In this poky court of jubilee.

So here's to paths that scratch and tease,
Where laughter lingers like a summer breeze.
In every scratch, a story to tell,
A bond we forge, oh so well.

Flavors of the Solstice

Under the sun, we roast and toast,
Berries dancing, we brag the most.
Jam spills over, sticky and bright,
As we feast into the delight of night.

Silly hats worn in the heat,
Boppy tunes that move our feet.
With every jar, we find our groove,
In this fruity fest, we shake and move.

A splash of laughter, a plate of cheer,
Each bite brings forth a silly tear.
As flavors meld into one great cheer,
In this wild season, our hearts steer clear.

So raise your spoons, let's sing and chime,
A harvest celebration, oh so prime.
With every drop, let the fun unfurl,
In flavors of summer, let's twirl and swirl.

The Thicket's Song

In a thicket wild and free,
Berries dance with glee,
A bushy chorus sings so loud,
Nature's own, unruly crowd.

Squirrels prance with berry treats,
Jays serenade from their seats,
Bramble thorns, a clumsy friend,
A fool's slide can make you bend.

The owls hoot a tune of cheer,
While raccoons pull up a chair,
A patch of laughter, a juicy bite,
Under the fading daylight.

So here's to every fruity prank,
Berry stains, a purple rank,
In the thicket, life's a dance,
Join the fun, give fate a chance.

Beneath the Berry Boughs

Under boughs, the laughter grows,
Sticky hands, it's how it goes,
Berries stain the cheek and chin,
Messy joy envelops in.

Bumblebees on faux pas roam,
Finding sweetness far from home,
With little feet, we leap and twirl,
Nectar dreams in summer's whirl.

Tangled vines, a game of chase,
A berry feast at our own pace,
Birds above chime in the play,
Making mischief every day.

As dusk descends, the giggles fade,
But memories in sunshine laid,
Below the boughs, the fun remains,
In berry patches, joy sustains.

Rhapsody of the Ripened

Ripened fruits bring wacky ways,
To gather them, we twist and sway,
A dance on toes, we reach and swing,
Nature's stage, our silly fling.

With every pluck, a plop and smear,
We're berry bandits, loud and clear,
Smitten smiles, our sticky fate,
In the line-up, we can't wait!

Frogs croak out their jealous jive,
While we dive and take the dive,
With pie in mind, we feast our eyes,
In this berry biz, we're the prize!

Laughter echoes through the glade,
As sunshine starts its slow parade,
The rhapsody of joy resounds,
Among the trees, our fun abounds.

The Glistening Dark

When night descends, the berries gleam,
A little light, a hidden dream,
The critters plot a midnight spree,
In shadows, wild and carefree.

Glistening dark, a funny sight,
With moonbeams serving up delight,
Sneaky paws and giggles rise,
As mischief glimmers in their eyes.

A berry band, a disco ball,
The thieving raccoons have a ball,
With bushes shaking, giggles loud,
They party hard—oh, what a crowd!

As dawn breaks soft on berry trails,
The tales of night turn into wails,
For berry buffs, both wild and sweet,
In morning light, they'll face defeat.

Whispers in the Bramble Field

In the bramble fields, we dance and sway,
Chasing after berries that roll away.
A laugh escapes, a tickle and tease,
As thorny branches scratch our knees.

Jars filled with jam, oh what a treat,
Sticky fingers and muddy feet.
We giggle and share our berry stash,
While squirrels plot to make a dash.

A picnic spread, but ants invade,
We leap and shout, not quite afraid.
A rogue berry flies, a splat on a hat,
We burst into fits, how about that?

With every bite of sweet delight,
We sing our songs until the night.
In the bramble field, our laughter rings,
A melody sweeter than any fruit brings.

Fruits of the Hidden Path

Down the hidden path where shadows play,
We find the fruits that lead us astray.
One too many berries, our heads feel light,
As we tumble and roll, oh what a sight!

The thorns are sharp, but we are brave,
Each snag and scrape, a memory to save.
A giant berry bounces, it leads the way,
And we chase it down, shouting hooray!

A critter scoffs at our berry quest,
With a twitch of his nose, he's one of the best.
He snags a few, while we take a tumble,
We join in the laughter, reflecting our fumble.

As dusk creeps on, our bounty we've crowned,
With eyes full of mischief, we spin around.
The fruits of our labor, all piled high,
With giggles and grub, we wave goodbye.

Murmurs of the Bramble Dream

In a bramble dream, where the wild things play,
Berries whisper secrets in a delightful way.
The moon blinks twice, and we chase a star,
While munching on fruits from close and far.

Bumblebees buzz like they know our fate,
While we wobble along, never too late.
A mischief of foxes joins in the fun,
As we dance and spin, 'til the day is done.

Thorns poke and prod, but we dance right through,
The sweeter the berry, the funnier too.
With laughter as loud as the rustling leaves,
We weave tales of tricksters and cheeky thieves.

As shadows stretch long, and twilight descends,
We gather our treasures, grateful for friends.
From every bramble, our memories gleam,
In this silly, sweet, and absurd bramble dream.

The Sweet Embrace of Shadows

In the shadows' embrace, where misfits collide,
We pluck at the berries that nature's supplied.
With giggles that echo like soft summer rain,
As we navigate thickets and sparkles of grain.

A thief steals a berry with crafty finesse,
Leaving us cackling in utter success.
We empty our pockets, with treasures we show,
As shadows dance lightly, putting on a show.

Our laughter a symphony, wild and free,
The berries, the thorns, and our wild jubilee.
In every sweet bite, a story unfolds,
Of sugar and spice, and a dash of bold.

So here in the silence, where whispers belong,
We savor the flavors, all luscious and strong.
The sweet embrace of shadows, our joy unabashed,
With each berry picked, our merriment's splashed.

Wild Harvests of the Night

In the moonlight, fruits are ripe,
With squirrels dancing, what a sight!
They tiptoe through the backyard maze,
Chasing shadows in a berry haze.

The jester's hat goes on the fence,
A raccoon struts, so nonchalant, hence!
With every pluck, we giggle and cheer,
As the wild harvest brings us near.

Beneath the stars, we laugh and roam,
Sticky fingers feel just like home.
The fruits of laughter fill the air,
With every bite, we lose all care.

Oh, berry knights in silly quests,
Battling thorns with laughter's jest.
On this wild night, our hearts unite,
In the harvest of pure delight!

Echoes of the Thorny Path

Stumbling down the prickly lane,
My friends and I, we're quite insane!
With every thorn a funny tale,
Of berry fights and epic flail.

One trip and tumble, I hit the ground,
As berries burst with joyful sound.
Laughter echoes off the trees,
In this wild romp, there's no unease.

A squirrel darts, we give pursuit,
Who knew that critter's life was cute?
With berry juice smeared on our cheeks,
The thorny path just adds mystique.

Here in the thicket, mirth prevails,
As jokes soar high like happy sails.
Every stumble fuels our glee,
In echoes of mischief, wild and free!

Whispers of the Midnight Fruit

Beneath the stars, a hush befalls,
The fruit sways gently, whispers calls.
A masked bandit steals a taste,
With berry juice, he makes haste.

The night is filled with giggling sounds,
As berry lovers twist around.
Each sweet bite sparks a silly cheer,
In the shadows, there's no fear.

With goblets raised of fruity blend,
We toast to laughter without end.
The whispers of the night grow bold,
As berry tales in mirth unfold.

A dance of shadows, a fruity fight,
In this midnight feast, all feels right.
Beneath the leaves, our joys take flight,
Whispers and giggles fill the night!

Serenade of the Twisted Vines

In the tangled vines, we take our stand,
With berry crowns and laughter planned.
The fruit sings soft, a playful tune,
While we sway beneath the moon.

Prancing pests like wild ballet,
Each berry bop is a grand display.
With every grab, a cheer erupts,
The tangled joy just interrupts.

Beneath the stars, we twirl and prance,
In this wild berry romancing dance.
With vines that twist, our worries fade,
In strawberry dreams, we serenade.

So raise your hands, let laughter soar,
In the serenade, we want more!
With every bite, a spark of cheer,
In twisted vines, we lose all fear!

The Enchanted Grove's Secrets

In a grove where shadows play,
Berries dance and sway all day.
They giggle in the golden light,
Whispering secrets, oh what a sight!

A squirrel sings with berries bright,
His acorn hat fits just right.
He twirls and hops, a funny dance,
Inviting all to share the chance.

The owls chuckle from the trees,
As bumblebees hum with the breeze.
Each berry holds a quirky joke,
They burst with laughter when you poke.

So gather 'round and take a bite,
Of fruity tales in pure delight.
In this grove, the fun won't end,
For each ripe berry is a friend!

Ballad of the Unseen Harvest

In the fields where shadows creep,
Lurking creatures laugh and leap.
They harvest fruits through giggles loud,
While the moonlight hides the crowd.

A tiny witch with a cheeky grin,
Sings to plants where fun begins.
Her broomstick dances on the ground,
As candy corn grows all around.

The ghosts play tricks on passing sheep,
Making sure they're wide awake and leap.
With every pluck of berry sweet,
There's laughter echoing beneath their feet.

So join the fun and share a smile,
For unseen harvests stretch for miles.
These giggling fruits will bring you cheer,
In the ballad sung to all who hear!

Feasting on Fables

Gather 'round for tales so grand,
With fruits and laughter hand in hand.
Each tale is flavored with delight,
A banquet born from day and night.

The crow tells secrets from the skies,
While raccoons feast with twinkling eyes.
They nibble on the stories spun,
Turning simple bites to fun!

A fox in glasses reads a book,
With every page, the berries cook.
Each chapter ripe, with funny twists,
Making sure no one can resist.

So take a plate, and join the spree,
For fables shared taste best, you see.
In every morsel, laughter spreads,
With all the joy that nature sheds!

Colors of Dusk and Delight

As the sun dips low, the colors play,
Fruits of laughter light the way.
With shades of purple and hints of gold,
Nature weaves a tale untold.

A parrot preaches with flair and fun,
Chasing shadows as they run.
In every berry, a joke is spun,
Promising delight to everyone.

The twilight sings with playful tones,
Mixing giggles with rolling stones.
From dusk's embrace, the laughter flies,
Painting smiles across the skies.

So taste the dusk, let flavors blend,
In colors where the laughter transcends.
With every bite, joy takes flight,
In the twilight's magical light!

www.ingramcontent.com/pod-product-compliance
Lightning Source LLC
Chambersburg PA
CBHW051654160426
43209CB00004B/892